THIRST:

A NOVELLA OF REDEMPTION

Thirst

A Novella of Redemption

Namaya

Published by:
Vermont Art Poetry Press
773 Guilford street
Brsttleboro, VT 05301
info@vermontartpoetry.com

Written by Namaya.

ISBN-13: 978-0-9990844-2-7
ISBN-10: 0-9990844-2-9

Printed in the United States of America

Larry Hamilton & the Vermont Veterans for Peace
for your tireless work for Peace.

TABLE OF CONTENTS

THIRST

In the year of our Lord 1420, during one of the many plagues that rose from the swamps and fed its appetite for the dead, a syphilitic fog slithered in from the swamps, crept like a stocking-footed thief along the back roads, wound its way through the gutters and city streets, nuzzled its face against the windowpane, sprang through a slender opening, and intermingled its breath with that of the sleeping. Each breath inhaled was a step closer to life for the deadly fog, and each breath exhaled was a minim of life lost. When the last breath was long expired, the corpse cold in the tomb, and the pale crescent moon shadowed in clouds, I would begin my work.

In time, I came to know more about the dead and dying than I did of life. Then, I believed, there was not that much to say about the dead; the soul has gone either to heaven or to hell and what remains is the shell: If the worms could claim the corpse--Why couldn't I? Did I always have to be a leather-maker, working with the stinking skins reeking of decay, my hands always red from the dyes? With a stench like that-- would Maria, the pretty servant girl whom I had loved since I was a boy, have me? Never! So I make my small fortune in the night and take my pleasures in the evening by the dock.

I am Pietro and, in 1420, when the night was ripe and perfect, the Grave Robber. When the anatomists needed a cadaver, I was only too happy to provide them with a woman, a child, or a man; it made no difference to me since one corpse was worth two weeks' wages. If I was fortunate and a wealthy patron was laid to rest, then a silver or gold cross was the added prize. The Jew silversmiths would not buy it because they knew it came from a grave. They would say, "We do not want to be part of Christian evil. Though we will be blamed for it, at least the blood will not be on our hands." The fat Friar Marco, who had always lived well despite his professed vows of poverty, had no such doubts. When the emerald- and jewel-encrusted cross was taken from the Bishop's cold, clawed hands, Marco paid me a handful of silver coins and blessed it: "I release this cross from its past and banish all evil that might have touched it."

Duke Lorenzo was not a Medici, though he lived like one with dozens of servants and teams of Arabian horses, in a granite castle perched on the barren hillside above the town. Of all the people who had succumbed to the plague that June, I thought he would escape. There was a rumor that the legendary sorcerer and master of the black arts Titus, who had learned his darkest secrets from the Moors of Granada, had cast spells to protect Lorenzo and keep him well.

I was near the silversmith's shop when Titus walked by, his wispy white beard making him appear more like a Duke than Lorenzo himself. He looked into my eyes and said, "Coins for your soul? Count the cost carefully."

"Pardon me, sir?"

"Consider the cost of silver. The price changes frequently here."

I looked at the silver coins he had dropped into my hand and then back at him. "What do you want?" Before I could finish my sentence, he was gone. I looked up and down the street, but there was no sign of him.

Lorenzo was at least eighty years old, yet he didn't appear a day older than sixty. Impossible! In 1420, more children died before their second birthday than there were people older than fifty. For a man to be sixty or more could only mean he had either the blessing of God or an equally powerful allay at his side. Did Titus hold such a power? I would not have known or guessed until that night. Despite the Duke's appearance of vitality, when the church bells rang and a black flag appeared over his castle, his mortality was certain.

It had been five days since his body had been laid to rest in an exquisitely polished white carrera marble tomb with the statues of St. Michael and St. Gabriel guarding the gates. The doors to the outer vault opened easily with a knife, and a slight creak sent a sent a chilling shiver through the calm night air. Two wolf-like dogs carved in black onyx guarded either side of the tomb. Carved on the foot of the sarcophagus was a star, a triangle, and a sentence that read, "Remove this lid and thirst for all time-- neither living nor dead." Foolish nonsense! But I crossed myself and said a prayer to my patron saint. If this were the tomb of the Black art, then God would protect me. I did not know what those words meant, but I remember them well, because I see them each night in what some might call sleep. The iron pry bar caught the lid and easily slid it open: whatever jewels or cross were buried with him would soon be mine. One of the onyx dogs moved and lowered its head. Was it only the shadow of the moon through the stained glass window? The second dog growled. Impossible! I had simply imbibed too much wine this evening. This would be the richest find and, on the grave of my mother, I swore this was the last tomb I would disturb. Tomorrow, I'd go to the cathedral and confess my sins, but first this work. As soon as the lid was pushed completely aside, light poured out of the tomb. The dog on the left suddenly leaped for my throat and the other sprang forward to devour my entrails. I felt their knife-like teeth ripping my flesh apart. Bleeding from a score of wounds, I fell into a fog of sleep. Soon, I knew, it would be over. "Forgive me. Forgive me," I whispered. Then there was only blackness: A dark feverish blackness.

I awoke in the morning inside the vault of Lorenzo. Sunlight streamed through the rose and violet windows. The sarcophagus lid was firmly in place. Now there was only one black marble dog at the foot of Lorenzo's tomb and at the base of was the inscription, *Natas*. A black wolf-like dog with eyes like burning coal lay beside me chained to my wrist. I opened my shirt and looked at my arms and chest, but there were no wounds; yet, my body was sore like I had been beaten. How was this possible? I remembered seeing myself bleed and feeling the dogs tear at my skin. Had God forgiven me and brought me back from the dead? I drew my hands up to pray, but no words came forth; only the taste of hot ashes on my tongue. The metal chain on my wrist rattled and as I reached for one of my knives to break the lock, the dog growled and lunged at me. When I stopped trying to separate myself from the dog or the lock, he was quiet. Who could free me from this? Was I still dreaming? Was I alive or dead?

With Natas firmly chained to my arm I went to the church, but when I tried to sneak in through the secret basement entrance known only to the whores and those who dared not walk through the front doors, the priest stopped me. "Without the dog, my son," he admonished me.

There was a sanctuary in the woods, a small shrine on the way to the river, and I was joyous to see the face of Jesus on the cross. When I came nearer on my knees, dragging Natas, the face of our savior became that of Natas and it snarled at me. I tried to scream, "Jesus, my savior! Forgive my sins. Jesus! Jesus!" But no words came out; there was only the taste of hot ashes on my tongue and a burning in my throat. Was there a word that could save me from my sin?

When it is night, though I'm exhausted and I should sleep, I close my eyes and live inside Natas. He roams through the woods, his nose sensing who and what is about to die. When an animal is killed in the woods, his nose is in the guts of the still bleeding animal, and he wants the heart while it is still beating, pulsating. He clenches his jaw around it and squeezes the life from it--that is the prize. In the morning, he's asleep beside me, yawns and looks at me with the playful innocence of a pup, but then I see those black eyes and it sends a cold fear through my soul.

Chained to the dog I followed him in dream, sleep, and waking: Wasn't that penance enough? Did I consider that I might break the chain? Maybe kill him? When you fear the dark, do you kill the darkness? When the wind rattles and breaks the branches off the tree, do you kill the wind? If I could kill Natas, I would gladly do it, but I couldn't.

I lived in a cave outside of town and every minute of my life was filled with the thought, "How do I become free?" Once I tried to poison myself with chemicals from the leather works. The acid burned down the center of my stomach and in the midst of the pain, I was joyful that I would die at last. Though I took enough poison to kill ten men, I didn't die. I awoke the next day, vomiting blood, which the dog lapped up, and I grew stronger.

"Damn, you!" I screamed, but no words came out. I silently prayed to die, but Natas dragged me out of the cave, ripped apples from the trees and dropped them on me. It was an order -- Eat! I ate ravenously and each night dreamed that I was Natas who wandered through the countryside feasting at the shallow graves or on the carcasses of the freshly killed animals. When he eats, I am stronger.

When war came to Padua, Natas and I followed the armies and the carnage in their wake. We would walk among the dead and dying at night. Soldiers would cry out and I would give them water and comfort. I tried to pray with them, but my lips couldn't make the sound – I was mute. I folded my hands and bowed my head, while Natas dug in the ground for a warm corpse beside us. When I prayed, he stopped feeding.

The Muslim army invaded Vienna in the 1600's. I walked among the heathen when the battle was over. The dying called out to Allah in their pain. Though some had a moment of fear, thinking that I was sent to slay them, most were too weak to move, and if I had come to kill them, then it would be a quicker end, but when I touched them, they knew. Their surgeons knew of the herbs to heal a dirty festering wound, but how does one heal the suffering of the soul or one who was dying?

Muslim battlefields gave way to the slaughter in the Crimea. More soldiers died from the rotting tins of meat, disease, and poisoned waters than from bullets. Handsome young men in beautiful scarlet uniforms with their trousers at their knees, shaking like feeble old men, poured out rivers of brown water. In a few months 30,000 soldiers-- English troops, Russian Cossacks, and Turkish Calvary -- had been killed. At the end of one battle, I tended to a twelve year-old drummer boy. The left side of his face was crushed and bleeding, the eye gone, part of the skull torn away, with the gray pudding of the brain pulsating and exposed. His iris blue eye was crying, as he beseeched me, "Bless me Reverend, for I have sinned." The prayer book in his pocket said his name was Mathew. I gave drops to the boy, not holy water, but hemlock and laudanum. Though I'm not a priest or a cleric, these battlefields are my church – with the putrid stench of death and disease, anointed with blood. "Matthew, you haven't sinned, but those who brought you here have," I comforted him.

I held him close to me and prayed with him till his last breath. "The lord is my shepherd…"

Then I went to the next person and the next. I reached as many as I could with a word and a potion. If God is good and just, He will take them swiftly, for whatever penance needs to be made, they surely made it here, dying alone on these fields. When there was time, I placed rocks over the bodies to make a simple grave. Most often the vultures feasted freely and the satanic angels soared to heaven with pieces of a body.

After the battles, the generals went back to their tents with their silk cushions and whores, and again fantasized of how they would annihilate the enemy. A chess game, with pawns moved around the board with no concern for the lives lost, or perhaps a game of dice, with fate decided solely by chance, rather than by skill.

For the first fifty years or so of this bondage, I never gave up hope that this chain would break or rust through. Though it weighed on me like a stone coffin, I realized that, by accepting this chain, no different than the cross that I had worn as a child, I was able to extract a small bit of peace.

Thoughts of freedom and, to a lesser extent, salvation, came as infrequently as rain in the desert, but when the rains do fall, the desert is blessed with a thrilling brush of green, bursts of vivid colors, and a carpet of fragrant lavender and sensuous purple flowers. So extravagant were my rare dreams of comfort.

But I am not a ghost or a phantom! I'm a man. I'm alive and famished for love, and I want to know the sweet caress of a woman, to be like other men, to have a wife and a child. I want to watch my children marry and have children of their own. I want to work during the day and at dusk drink wine with my friends at the tavern, and never hear another cannon or see pieces of a boy scattered on a battlefield. Is this the lesson: Thy will be done? If so, what is Thy will?

The night that Mathew died, I dreamed I was in a large limestone Neapolitan villa by the sea. The waves didn't pound or crash against the rock; they met like famished lovers and the sky spread wide open like a lonely widow ready for love. Natas was a graying dog with a white muzzle, toothlessly gnawing and licking a dry ox bone. Soldiers, camp followers, and children, maimed by a bullet or a spear, came to the table. Mathew was there, not as a boy, but as a strong handsome young man and we embraced. I remember each soldier I held, though I rarely knew anyone's name, and though, in most cases, I didn't speak their language. Now I could greet each by their name, in their own tongue, and converse with ease and hear the story of their life before the war. We feasted together at this great round table of many languages. There was spring water from the Italian Alps, Tuscan red wine, freshly baked rye and barley bread, honey from Crete, olives and oranges from Spain. We joined hands, bowed our heads, and gave thanks –for being able to sit at this table: Jew, Muslim, Christian, and yes, Pagan - those who found their God in the forests and beneath the wide shelter of the sky. When I spoke our common prayer, of joy and gratitude, my voice was strong. My tongue could say the words that I heard in my heart, and where before my tongue tasted like hot ashes, there was a coolness and ease as we gave thanks.

In the Battle of the Marne, in the war that was to end all wars, it was a sea of muddy red craters, and the primal forests that stretched from horizon to horizon that abounded with deer, rabbits, foxes, and paradise itself -- all of it was gone -- only the blackened stumps of the few oaks remained. With scarcely a tree or a blade of grass to slow it down, the wind scoured across the fields.

The whistle from the sergeant pierced the air, "Over the top, lads!" The enemy's machine gun fire was steady, "For God, Country, and King." Knowing that half the men would be killed, they still blindly followed the order, "Across the fields!" The shrill of a thousand shells whined across the skies, tearing bodies apart and scattering limbs. The boys fell like ripe stalks of wheat felled by a just-sharpened scythe. Dressed as soldiers, convinced that this was what they must do if they were real men, many were from a small village outside of Surrey. They had grown up together, played war games in the meadows and lush rolling cow pastures, and dreamed of glory in the real war, when it came: Today, as the battle came to an end, there was no glory, only boys lying buried in the cold mud, dead and dying. When the blue crescent moon cast a pale luminescent glow across the battlefield, I envisioned them as they rose from the mud, returned home, married their sweethearts, fathered a brood of children, became fat and successful, and died at home at a ripe old age surrounded by children, grandchildren, and great grandchildren. The image of this full, long life vanished when the boy I was holding died in my arms. All of his children and grandchildren disappeared and began to look for a different future. The soldier's sweetheart married the clubfooted carpenter who hadn't been able to march off to war. One day, from a distance of about thirty meters, I saw a woman holding a soldier. Her hair was thick, white, and lustrous, drawn back with a black ribbon. She turned to me with a serene smile revealing a face that was smooth, but aged like well-worn leather. She appeared both young and old at the same time. When the soldiers looked in her eyes, did they see their beloved or their mothers? She stayed with the one soldier for hours, holding his head next to her breast, stroking his hair, and giving him fresh water. When it was time for him to leave she kissed him on his forehead as a mother might kiss a sleeping child, bidding him, "Goodnight, sleep well."

I had seen her before in Crimea sixty years ago, walking among the wounded soldiers, offering comfort and water. Today as she sat on the ground with the soldier, I saw his spirit leave his body. It was good to see him as he was before the war. She took his hand and walked with him towards the sunrise, and then he was gone.

I've seen a few others tending the sick and the dying, but none like myself, with Natas. I no longer remember being without him. We wake, sleep, and eat together. He is as much part of me as my right arm, as essential as my heart. In the beginning, I cursed my fate, but in every fate there is a blessing. In every task in life there is a blessing and a curse: Which do you embrace? By embracing one and not the other, do you fail to hold the full measure? When there is a war about to begin, no matter how long Natas and I have been in one place, I gather my bedroll, my diary, and my bible, and I walk where he leads.

When the last shell was launched, and after the millions of German, English, French, Africans, Indian and scores of other nationalities were killed, did anything change? Did someone become right? Who was wrong? In the millions who were killed, was there one who would have painted a picture on par with the best Renaissance artist? Was there a genius who would have discovered the cure for war? Or was there a poet who could explain this insanity?

Along a barbed wire fence, a clown dressed in white with a small red hat, a white painted face, and a red bulbous nose peddled by on his unicycle. With every toot of his horn, up rose a child -- English, German, and Italian, some dressed in school uniforms with smart little caps. They followed behind the clown. Some had penny whistles, others tambourines, and one boy had fashioned a drum from the helmet he'd worn a few hours earlier. The clown honked, and the children lined up, following in a little parade till they reached the edge of the horizon and vanished.

Why are we drawn to war? Why do we feast on hate and fear? In these centuries alone with Natas, he pulls me forward to each battlefield, and forces me to see. The dog mocks me. He walks with me among the dead. He seems to say, "Look! Look! See!" He seeks the warm blood and I look to be anointed by the tears of the soldiers. Are we always chained to our violence? What breaks the link between man and the demon?

One night in late November, after the last shell had been fired, there was a feeling of exhaustion, as if neither side could give one more man, and no mother or wife could possibly cry one more tear. Everything was exhausted and depleted: the earth, the air, the poisoned water, and the soldiers, weary to the core of their being. Even the thought of getting up and walking home felt almost impossible. One soldier was leaning against another and, realizing that his gun was too heavy, threw it aside. The sergeant saw this and was about to shout an order, but the words never left his mouth, and soon every soldier in the company did the same. With a heavy thud the guns sank slowly into the mud. Soon the sergeant would be back in the steel mills of Sheffield, his soldiers beside him. Would the pounding of the mills and the blast of the hot furnace muffle the memory of five years in hell? What could bring a soldier home to the life he knew before?

I saw the old woman and she was sitting alone on a tree stump with her hands folded, looking out over the fields. This was the same woman. Yes, the very same woman. Her face was covered in dirt and her fingernails were ragged and broken.

"Pietro, at last we meet again," She said to me.

"You can't be..."

"Have you forgotten me?"

In kinship we had walked these fields, never touching or meeting until now. Could it be? She looked like Maria, the servant girl I had loved, but that would be impossible! Three hundred years later? I had come to believe that I was dead, more ghost than man.

"What could cause you to be here?" I asked her.

"You know that neither one of us decided our fate," she replied.

"I was with my husband when the soldiers came through town. There was one fine, tall sergeant, with a bright red beard, and he could make me laugh like no other. For five years I had been with my husband, who was old and afflicted with skin pustules and the stench of onions. I was prideful and vain, and one moonlit night I followed my soldier. We lived like gypsies, and for a short while I was joyous, because I was at last in love and had so longed to be free. Soon I was cooking and laundering for the soldiers. When they were defeated at the Po River, my soldier was killed on the first day of battle and I was captured by the Genoans. I was bought and sold by a roll of the dice. When my new master, the young Captain was wounded, I cared for him with herbs and oils, and he freed me, but I stayed because I had nowhere to go. I was the woman with the herbs who stopped the bleeding with salves that healed the festering wounds, and the oils that soothed the fevers, and the roots that gave the soldiers calm. When the plants spoke and the soldiers heard, they got well, and when the wounds were too great, the herbs gave them peace. My simple medicines were yarrow for wounds, nightshade and elder for fevers, boneknit to mend, and agrimony for the stomach...but you know this. I have watched you comfort the soldiers, even with the unspeakable one chained to you."

"But you're not chained like I? You can leave, yes?"

"Yes, I could leave, but who would care for them? And you, Pietro? How have you been?" She reached over and caressed my face.

I had not heard my Christian name in hundreds of years. It was as if all the centuries had disappeared and the year was 1420 again, before Natas and the wars.

"Come, Pietro, lie down with me."

We drew the two cots together and lay on the woolen, moth-eaten, olive green blankets. In the open womb of the trench, we held each other. In the middle of this sea of mud and pain where, for five long years, millions had died, there was scarcely a sound as the wind rolled like a whisper across the land. To be able to hold another person, who wasn't dying or sick, gave me a feeling of exquisite peace. The stars came out, and we huddled close together in the cold night, and spoke in the language of our village, a language I had almost forgotten. And I remembered the simple joy of holding someone you were in love with.

"But the dog? Natas?" she asked me.

"Yes, he will be quiet," I assured her.

In the hours of holding her, it seemed as if Natas slipped away. We lay there, listening to the absolute silence, save for one very distant bird calling, as if searching for her mate. No soldiers. No one dying. We embraced in the stillness. I felt the ghostness of my life disappear and the man who I once was emerged. We made love with the freshness of two virgins and a gratitude that only the old can truly comprehend.

I awoke in the morning to the sound of booming thunder on the horizon. A bolt of lightening ripped through the black clouds that hovered above us.

"Is it time for us to leave?"

"It is time."

"Together?"

"No, Pietro. We will meet again, I'm sure of it."

She stood up, straightened out her long brown woolen dress and combed back her thick white hair and tied it with a black ribbon. She kissed me on the lips. "God bless you for your good works," she whispered. "He hears your prayers."

"But what about Natas?"

She turned to the East as lightning bolts again stabbed across the sky that were so large I felt they would pierce the very heart of the earth. She said quietly, "Yes, I know about Natas. Remember, God hears every one of your prayers and may His peace abide with you." She made the sign of the cross and walked to the East, towards the boarder of Poland. I watched her till she reached the edge of the field. As she waved goodbye, her smile was a loving benediction.

That night I fell to sleep and dreamed I was Naples. I slept on pressed linen sheets, bathed in lavender and rosewater, and had my body massaged with almond and olive oil. In this dream I was free of Natas. I savored the peace of sitting in the sand, enchanted by the sunlight as it played a symphony of diamond notes on the crest of each rolling wave.

Then I awoke and I was now in Asia. The Vietnamese nationalists fought against the Japanese, rescued American flyers, modeled their constitution on that of the Americans, declared their independence, and were then betrayed as their country again fell under the rule of the French. When the French were defeated, the Americans and their allies followed, but they would also taste the bitterness of hubris and defeat.

For days I followed a path that snaked up higher into the mountains, where the clouds embraced the peaks. Was there someone who needed to be comforted? Why this long route? We had just been near Hue where thousands of villagers had been displaced and caught between the Americans - who promised freedom, but who burned the villages - and the North Vietnamese - who promised a country, but took their sons and daughters as soldiers. American soldiers killed women and children, afraid that they were the enemy. I had thought I neither would nor could cry ever again, but after the soldiers left, I sobbed as I buried the children and their parents in simple common graves. One girl was about five years old with large brown eyes, long dark lashes, and a full, round face. She clutched a thin pink plastic doll to her chest. Was she trying to protect the doll, or holding it close for comfort as the bullet ripped open her stomach? I closed the little girl's eyes, and laid her and her doll on the ground next to her parents. "May you live to be healthy, wise, and old in your next life. May God bless you." The words came from my heart, paused on my tongue, and caressed my lips. But there was no tenderness; only anger that I shouted to the ears of God Himself: "Bless and embrace this child!" I could only wish for the future, as there was nothing here. For three days I stayed in the village that was now little more than a field of blackened houses. Back where the jungle started to encroach on the fields, I positioned the graves in a circle, with Mother, Father, and child together. There was an old man, gnarled and bent over with age, who was bayoneted to death at the other end of the village. I buried him with that family. On the third day, at dusk, I was finished. Though there were still tears that never came, I raised my head to the skies and clasped my dirt-blackened hands together in prayer. After five-hundred years, Natas no longer begrudged my prayers. He was the truer saint for me, may God not strike me for that; he knew the false words that had once rolled off my tongue, but when the prayers came from the heart, they were conveyed directly to the heavens, and not even Natas could stop it.

The helicopters were coming our way, and they landed in the center of the barren land where the village had stood. A hungry puppy came from out of a wooden hut and started yelping, hoping that they would feed him. A short clip from the US soldier's' M-16 silenced him. The forest birds burst through the trees. Natas snarled and would have ripped out the throat of the young Lieutenant, but I held him close and we disappeared into the jungle, leaving the Americans in the blackened village.

Some several hundred meters to the north, by the narrow dirt road that led out of the village, wheeling around on a wobbly bicycle, was the white-faced clown with the bulbous nose, wearing a white suit and a red hat, blowing on a penny whistle. He weaved his way through the graves where I had buried the families, and up they rose, smiling and holding hands while blowing whistles of their own to chase away the evil spirits. Then I saw the back of one helicopter burst into flames and the soldiers were flung into the air from the blast. The clown bicycled through the remains of the village, near the burning helicopter, and a long line of children, American and Vietnamese, followed him as he left on the northern road and disappeared into the jungle.

I walked across the central highlands, in the cool mountaintop forests with parrots darting through the air in bursts of scarlet and satin green, with the echoing calls of hundreds of birds ricocheting through the dense, leafy-green jungle-world. The short staccato of the chicom rifles, and the steadier rip of the Browning automatic, caught my ear in the distance, and then faded. I could distinguish who was advancing and who was retreating, the difference between the new soldiers and the veterans, and who would likely soon die and who might survive.

The valley below, in the wide stretches of the Mekong Delta that had arisen hundreds of thousands of years ago, was now contested in a daily battle that ebbed and flowed with a tide tinted in blood. We rested in the mountains and there was, at least for the time being, some calm and peace, as the gunfire suddenly stopped, and the Viet Cong slipped back into their jungle lair.

Near the peak of the mountain was an old Buddhist temple with stone walls matted with dark green moss. The walls were broken and shattered, with vines snaking through the cracks, but the statue of the Buddha was undisturbed, and fresh flowers--hibiscus and jungle orchids--were placed all around the base where several candles were burning. I folded my hands and bowed to the Buddha. From the broad green leaves of the trees I made my bedding, and my torn, soiled linen coat was my pillow. There was peace for a moment in this mountain sanctuary. Not a sound of gunfire or war for miles around. I took no comfort, as the sounds were always with me and I knew how close each rifle or gunshot was, who fired it and how, and whether there was fear or panic. I know these sounds intimately; they are more familiar to my ear than are the names of birds and they are far more familiar than that one sound I most longed for--the haunting silence that comes after the war is over--like the silence that reigned the night Maria and I lay together. I took an orchid and placed it between Natas' iron collar and chain. He shook it loose and it fell to the earth. He sniffed it and ate it. Faithful friend! No, neither friend nor faithful, but my persistent teacher. He lets me choke on each false word and every insincere act.

Curled at the base of the Buddha in the ruins of the shrine, I finally fell asleep and embraced the uncertain peace that sleep brings. Each sleep brings a journey. I sailed across the mountains to the fields of Cambodia, and it looked like the same broad savanna along the banks of the Mekong Delta. The children were maimed; some were in wheelchairs, some were burned, and others had wooden legs crudely carved from tree limbs. A general, with a chest full of medals and a strong jutting jaw, saw a child without legs, bent down on his knees, removed his hat with gold braid, folded his hands and beseeched the child, "Please, forgive me for what I've done." He had ordered landmines placed in this area and now the land was saturated, the mines hidden in the fields and along the roadside, waiting to strike again. He sat down on the ground, removed his own right and left leg prostheses, and gave them to the child. The boy placed them on the stumps where his legs used to be. In my dream, the man-sized legs shrank to fit the boy perfectly. A wheelchair was brought out for the general, and the child helped him into it and said thank you.

The soldiers and officers who had planted the landmines lined up and, one by one, asked the children for forgiveness. The lines stretched for several miles. One child, Noh, had been blind for five years and had been led around by his brother. He would ask him how the trees changed from year to year, what the color was of the river in Spring, and what the sun looked like each day. Hearing about this miracle, he finally came face to face with the soldier who placed the landmines in the garden next to his house. The soldier knelt in front of him, touched his head to the ground, and gave the boy his left eye. The soldier was only fifteen, a few years older than Noh, and he was crying. Noh said, "If I let you keep the other eye, will you do something for me?"

"Anything you ask. Anything at all," said the weeping soldier.

"Travel the country, find the landmines, tell others where they are, and remove them. When you're not able to remove them, build fences around them so that no person or animal will be hurt as they walk across it."

In turn, each soldier passed on the message: "No more land mines and no more war." With the help of the children, they spread throughout the country to find all the old mines.

I awoke in the morning with a deep sense of calm and clarity. An old monk in worn saffron-colored robes came to me with green tea and a basket of fruit. "Welcome," he said. "I'm grateful that you're here."

The monk told me the history of the monastery. He said that in the last century it had been a center for healing where nuns and monks prayed and cared for the sick. It was an oasis of peace until an invading army came and destroyed it. Though little remained, many from the local villages still came to offer prayers and alms. I understood why I had turned down the road to come to this place—it was to find the children in my dream. Though nothing would replace the eyes stolen from a child, or give back the pleasure of dancing to a child without legs, we could offer hope and some help. At first we were able to help only a few, but when the word spread that there was a place for children to come, where they could be fitted for new arms and legs made of wood or plastic, they began to come in a steady flow, that soon turned into a current, like that of a river. The blind children were taught to use their other senses fully "to see," as the lepers, with deformed, mangled hands, showed the children how to weave beautiful cloth. Soldiers crippled by war, without family or home, showed the children how to use their crutches and new limbs. The children – maimed, shocked, mute, joyless, or homeless – all of them made their way to our sanctuary. The old monk called this place *Compassion*, and in my prayers I asked for a blessing for the village, which I called *Forgiveness*. Perhaps, Compassion and Forgiveness are the same.

I stayed long after the fall of Saigon and thought that finally this would be home. The calm of the sanctuary, with the chanting prayers of the Buddhist monks and the laughter of the children playing in the courtyard, brought a deep joy to my soul. This was my work and I wanted nothing more of life than to stay here, but I was surprised to again fall asleep. Why? What is the greater wisdom that constantly pushes me forward? I woke up in the USA. How strange to be there. I'd known the Yankees in the Great War and the Asian wars, but the idea of living among them was curious to me. Why this one town? I did not smell war or death here. During the Revolutionary War, there had been a minor battle in this small southern Vermont town, when a bunch of local farmers had chased some soldiers. Those who died were long gone, but I don't believe in ghosts; only people with unfinished tasks.

I walked along the river, out to a dirt road where I found an empty cottage with a sign on it that said "Caretaker wanted." Yes, I am a caretaker. I removed the sign, cleaned the house, and moved the garbage outside. Later that afternoon a young man came by.

"Hi, I'm John. I live next door. Are you the new caretaker?" he asked.

He had light brown skin, green eyes with folds that looked Asian, and a soft, familiar smile. Somewhere I had seen that face before -- perhaps with a slightly darker complexion and a different texture to the hair. Then I recalled a blinded American soldier I'd led out of the jungle of Laos in 1967. "Pablo?" I asked.

"No, as I said, I'm John. Pablo was my father's name. Did you know him?" He looked strangely at me and Natas who sat quietly.

I hadn't spoken English in a long time, but I had known many Americans during the war, and the language rolled easily off my tongue. I startled John by tossing out a couple idiomatic phrases, just for fun: "What's happening, man? Damn, it's a groovy spring."

"What? Where did you learn your English?" he asked with surprise.

"From my buddies in Saigon. You dig my English?"

"Sure, but it's so much like listening to my dad and to his friends."

Then I realized that maybe I didn't quite have the local dialect correct. "I'm sorry, it's been a while since I used English, but you can dig what I'm saying?"

"Of course. I uh, dig... Your English is a little... far out. Were you a soldier in Vietnam?"

"No, I was a... a caretaker of sorts. Is this your house?"

"Actually, my dad used to live here. Did you know him?"

"I knew many soldiers in Vietnam."

John told me about his father Pablo who had died three months before,and how he had been sick for most of his life from the chemicals used in the war. When I first saw chemicals sprayed from helicopters, and the way they made the trees wither, I understood why the newborn babies were deformed and why so many people became sick.

In the following weeks, I went to the Veterans Hospital during the day and at night spent time with John and his family. On my daily rounds at the hospital, I passed out fresh water and candy and had time to talk with the men. Some of these men had been there at the front, facing live fire, but quite a number were dying from drug addiction and years of neglect.

"You!" a voice shouted from behind me.

I turned to face an old man who must have been close to one-hundred years old. He was sitting up in bed, having ripped off his facemask for breathing.

"You, Father!"

I tried to leave, but he called again. "I know you! You were there at the Battle of Chantilly Woods! August 4, 1918. You were there with that same black dog. I had been gassed and you dragged me away from the open fields. Then you went back for my friends, with that dog, until the last man was safely behind the front lines."

Like a row of cards in a file box, my mind turned back to that day. I looked at this shrunken old man, skinny and frail, and as I approached him I saw that his eyes were still a vibrant green. I had known him when he was a young man six feet tall and well-muscled.

"It is good to see you again, my friend. It's been much too long."

Natas sprawled on the cool hospital floor and I sat on the edge of the bed to speak to Charley. "If it weren't for you," he said, "all of us in that squad would have been killed. You could have died, each time you went back, but you didn't stop--not till everyone was gone. When we got back, we tried to find you. We told everyone about you and many others had told a story about you and the dog. I wanted to thank you for the longest time, but I could never find you." He also spoke of his life, the wife who died in childbirth, the years of grieving for her, and then living alone on the city streets.

"Father, is it time to go?"

"My friend, you know I'm not a priest. I'm just like you."

"No, you're more angel than man and now I know why I've waited so long to die. It was to see you. Thank you."

"Sir, Mr. Johnson needs his sleep and he's not wearing his oxygen mask. You know volunteers aren't supposed to interfere with patient treatment."

I looked up at the young nurse, past the stern look, and saw a familiar spark in her eye. How the universe offers us a surprise at each turn of the day.

"Yes, Maria."

"How did you know my name was Maria? I don't have my name tag."

"You have the face of a girl from Padua, in Italy. Actually, a small village about a few miles from there. Right?"

"I'm not sure of the town. Do we know each other?"

"Actually, I knew your grandmother, of sorts."

"Maria! Maria!" called out another patient. She sprinted over to help that patient, who was trying to rip out his IV and climb out of bed.

I turned to Charley Johnson. His eyes, wet with tears, looked upwards, and then at me. "Is it time to go? And if it is time, then let me say again, thank you for being there. But how are you so young? You look like you're only seventy. When I saw you last, maybe you were sixty. Oh, of course, I should know, you're...."

"No, Charley. You only have to leave when you're ready."

"Then hear my confession."

"Charley, there is nothing to confess. You've been a good man all your life, devoted to your wife. You did the best you could and there is nothing to forgive. Travel well and may God bless and keep you safe." He breathed quietly, with a small smile on his lips and I closed his eyes.

"Come, Natas."

We walked the road that evening and I could feel the presence of Charley walking beside me, not as an old man, but as healthy young fellow, lightly skipping along the road, and it was good to hear him laugh. When the road changed from pavement to dirt, my small white cottage was there. The wind shifted slightly and Charley was gone.

Home. For the traveler, no matter how far he has wandered, there is no sweeter word than home. The rain fell with a slight chill and the winds from the north swept across trees, spraying a mist of yellow pollen on the lush green fields. After lighting the wood stove, I stuffed a bit of fresh-cured tobacco into my pipe and lit it, and I wrote while Natas fell asleep by the fire. Though the chain was attached to my arm, it was as much a part of me as my skin, and it never stopped me from believing or writing. Though fountain pens are a marvelous invention, I am too accustomed to my quill. However, it is easier than mixing the ink, paring down the nib of the quill, and drying the page. I prefer the familiar to the unknown and new.

JOHN'S NARRATIVE

Who was this man? This question has haunted me since he left. Though he was here for almost six months and spent a few hours every evening playing with my children, I felt I should have known him better. At first it seemed bizarre that this man was chained to the dog, but with his poor eyesight he obviously needed a guide; yet, I became suspicious when I saw him walk through the woods and he seemed like he was leading Natas. Was he what he appeared to be: a kindly old man with a black German shepherd?

I recalled one of many conversations: "Peter," I said, "I've seen a lot of people with seeing-eye dogs, but I've never seen someone who was so close to their dog."

"Natas and I are like the right and left side," said Peter. "He is my left side and I am his right. You're right that we rarely leave each other's side. One night I thought he had escaped and I had no idea where he'd gone, but the next morning he came back, and he was slinking, as if had done something shameful."

Several weeks before he left, on a cool overcast June afternoon, Peter was tending the flowers in his yard, and I was fixing the fence in front of the house. An elderly couple drove up to the house. They appeared lost. Their English was so poor that I couldn't help them, but

Peter was listening and said, "John, I might be able to help." Without pause he spoke to them in what sounded like Arabic,and they were thrilled. We all had had tea in the garden, and I saw that Peter was always pulling the dog back very gently, as if he were restraining it. When they got up to go to their car, the elderly man petted the dog and said something like, "Shaitan." Natas snarled and barked, and if Peter hadn't had such a firm grip on the dog, he probably would have bitten the man's hand.

"I'm sorry." Peter said. "Natas always displays his worst manners at the oddest of times. Please forgive him. I think he is becoming old, or as you say, 'senile.' Bad dog!" If he hadn't been chained to Peter, Natas would have slunk away with his tail between his legs.

As our visitors were leaving, they said to Peter and me, "Thank you for the tea and helping us. You're very kind, but that dog is darkness." And they headed back up the road.

"Armenian," Peter said to me. "I picked up a little bit of it along the way. I was, well, I got around when I was younger. "

When my son, Joshua, was doing his French homework, I heard Peter explain the lesson to him in what sounded like fluent French. In a few months Joshua was easily conversing in French.

I asked him about his profession and what he'd done when he was younger, and he replied, "A little of this and a little of that. I was at one time a peddler and then, for a long time, I was a—caretaker. You learn a lot when you travel, but as to formal studies, if that's what you are asking me—no, I didn't have the opportunity."

"When my friend Professor Giancarlo was here, you switched to Italian, and then, he said for fun, he switched to Renaissance Italian, and he said you spoke it like a native. Then he got very curious and spoke to you in Medieval Latin. You couldn't have learned that on the road!"

Peter roared with laughter, "Is that what he was talking? I did lose him for a while and, truthfully, I didn't have the heart to stop him since he was having such a good time. John, what was that movie? The one we saw the other night, with the idiot gardener? 'Being There'? That's the same thing. I know a little in a few languages. I smile a lot and pay close attention to the spirit of the conversation. You have a vivid imagination and you give me too much credit." With that he tousled my hair like I was a little boy. "Don't read so many books or believe fairy tales. They'll confuse you."

"Seriously, even if you never went to school, you've had a long life and seen a great deal of the world. Out of all the things you've learned, what is the most important?"

Without pause, Peter looked directly into my eyes and said, "Kindness."

You always wonder about a stranger. He could have been a murderer or a child-molester, but those light brown eyes had a sparkle and clearness that one rarely saw. You were almost sure that he was neither, but one rarely knows anything for certain, and what I discovered in the following week made me realize how little I really did know about him.

Natas played and frolicked with my children. Though he was always on a chain, he didn't appear to mind it, as though it were part of that which he was. Peter sometimes appeared as if he were miles away sitting in the chair, but he would hold the chain securely and roll it around in his fingers. He seemed attuned to every thought that Natas had. Once, when he was sitting there, little Sarah tumbled over and seemed to strike Natas on the head. Peter instantly woke up with a start and tensed on the leash. Natas lay there and whimpered. "Good dog, Natas. Very good." As Peter stroked Natas's head, the dog gave a low rumble in his throat that was like the purr of a satisfied kitten than a growl.

I was expecting Peter to come over that evening for supper, and when he didn't show up, I walked over to his cottage. Usually, he was by the roadside each day walking with Natas, tending to the herb and flower garden. I went inside the house. It was a very simple layout: a table, a few chairs, and flowers in a rusted milk can on the table.

"Peter? Are you in? Peter?" I pushed open the door to the one bedroom, and he was lying there on his cot, very still.

"Who's there?"

"Peter, what's wrong? It's John. What happened to you? Where is Natas?" It was strange. Seeing Peter without Natas was like seeing someone without legs.

"When I awoke this morning, he was gone. I had a dream that I was walking down a road that looked like it would never end, and then I reached the edge of a cliff and he was gone. What will I do? Where shall I go?"

He must have had a stroke or maybe the shock of losing his life-long companion had made him disoriented. Like many people, his dog was his life, and it was unfathomable that he would ever leave. How could one leave their master or the master leave the dog?

"Come home with me, Peter. You shouldn't be alone. Stay with us. The children love being with you and I can take off the chain."

He looked at me and then at the right arm with the bracelet, as if suddenly it dawned on him that he was no longer chained to Natas. "My arm feels so light, and it's strange not being with him. He was my guide, my shepherd--and he taught me…everything. Even when he repulsed and sickened me…he taught me what it was to be human. Do you understand?"

No, I didn't understand what he was talking about. It was the ramblings of a very old man who had lost his life-long companion. "You probably put the chain on because you thought Natas would get lost. Don't worry, it'll be good to have you stay with us. You shouldn't be alone."

"No, Natas put the chain on me so I wouldn't get lost."

There was no point in arguing and we walked out of the house. He took his bible in his left hand. The right arm, newly liberated, still bore the bracelet and a small length of chain.

"Thank you for taking me home, John." He took firm hold of my right arm and we walked up the road.

I felt myself grow lighter and lighter with a sense of peace and calm that I had never know before. He held me close, like when my father would walk with me as a child, and I felt absolutely safe, even on the darkest of nights. Though it was a clear dusk, I saw someone walking ahead, growing slightly larger, and then a gust of a wind swept across the road. When the dust cleared, I was confused to realize that Peter was gone. No one was behind me or in front of me. It started to rain—full, thick raindrops. I was thirsty and opened my mouth wide to drink, and it was sweet. He was gone. I walked back to the bend in the road and noticed a rusted ring with thick links in the grass beside the road; the last one was broken. An old woman came towards me, with thick white hair, wearing a long brown dress. Her face was deeply wrinkled, but she had a comforting smile. "Excuse me, sir," she said. "Did you see my friend, Pietro? I was supposed to meet him here tonight."

"Do you mean Peter?"

Something caught my attention and I turned to look behind me.

"Yes, Pietro."

Then I was alone.

EPILOGUE

I returned to Peter's cottage on the following day to see if I could make sense of what had happened the night before. On his desk were several small, yellowed parchment and vellum books. The writing was in an archaic script, possibly Latin or Italian, and I asked my friend, Professor Giancarlo from the University, to translate it for me. The last entry said, "I am old--many years old. Have these wars taught me anything? Will the thousands of people I have held offer me a grain of wisdom or peace? There are more wars to come, and soon I will go. For the hours that I've been here with John and his family, free of death, pain, and illness, I've found peace. Though I've found comfort in learning to forgive the leaders and generals, I cannot truly understand their hatred and greed that caused the wars and violence. Natas may one day leave, but the questions will remain. In my quest for repentance and salvation I am no different from the warriors; we are yoked together with the same burden, and that is to be human, though our paths to answer that quest are far different. In each one of us there is the thirst for immortality, and a greater thirst for love and union with God. Which do we hear the loudest, our vanity or the voice of heaven? My thirst was for forgiveness, and I could gain that only when I learned to forgive others. So simple! Yet, this heart had once been like stone, cold and unmoving. Tears, mine and those of the soldiers I've held, have been like the constant roll of the surf that wears away the coarsest of stone, until it is dissolved and becomes one with the sand. This thirst for peace abides."

I turned to the beginning of the book and read the first line: "In the year of our Lord 1420, during one of the many plagues that rose from the swamps..."

Namaya
©2004

www.ingramcontent.com/pod-product-compliance
Lightning Source LLC
Chambersburg PA
CBHW071227130626
46555CB00004B/1879